CLIMATE
CHANGE:
OUR IMPACT ON EARTH

HABITAT DESTRUCTION

by

Harriet Brundle

KidHaven
PUBLISHING

Published in 2018 by
KidHaven Publishing, an Imprint of Greenhaven Publishing, LLC
353 3rd Avenue
Suite 255
New York, NY 10010

Designer: Drue Rintoul
Editor: Charlie Ogden

Photocredits
Abbreviations: l-left, r-right, b-bottom, t-top, c-center, m-middle.

Front Cover: tr – Mindscape studio, tl – Tischenko Irina, br – exopixel, b – Nik Merkulov, lm – hanohiki. 4b – Matt Berger. 4tr – Jinga. 4bl – ThisNight. 5br – Jacek Fulawka. 6t – Ghiglione Claudio. 6m – DonLand. 6b – Brian Kinney. 7t (l–r) – JFs Pic Factory, Bildagentur Zoonar GmbH, OKAWA PHOTO, Cristian Gusa, Michal Ninger. 7br – David Peter Ryan. 7bl – Petri Volanen. 8 – Rich Carey. 9t – Chayanin Wongpracha. 9b – Gallinago_media. 10t – Nico Traut. 10b – idiz. 11 – Gino Santa Maria. 12 – Tyler Olson. 13t – Mary Terriberry. 13b – Ilona Koeleman. 14t – Jamie Hall. 14b – Ivan_Sabo. 15 – Darryl Brooks. 16t – Fabio Lamanna. 16b – Polina Shestakova. 17 – Fotos593. 18t – SvedOliver. 18b – Christophe Cappelli. 19t – acro_phuket. 19b – Jolanta Wojcicka. 20r – Aditya Singh. 21 – shama65. 22bl – LMspencer. 23c – Smileus. 23tr, 23br – PRILL. 24 – Seaphotoart. 25t – Gleb Tarro. 25b – Jezper. 26tr – bjul. 26b – Ovchinnikova Irina. 27t – adike. 27b – Vanatchanan. 28t – wavebreakmedia. 28m – Diego Cervo. 28b – bikeriderlondon. 29t – kay roxby. 29m – Poznyakov. 29b – stefanolunardi. Images are courtesy of Shutterstock.com, with thanks to Getty Images, Thinkstock Photo, and iStockphoto.

Cataloging-in-Publication Data

Names: Brundle, Harriet.
Title: Habitat destruction / Harriet Brundle.
Description: New York : KidHaven Publishing, 2018. | Series: Climate change: our impact on Earth | Includes index.
Identifiers: ISBN 9781534524699 (pbk.) | 9781534524439 (library bound) | ISBN 9781534524705 (6 pack) | ISBN 9781534524446 (ebook)
Subjects: LCSH: Habitat conservation–Juvenile literature. | Habitat (Ecology)–Juvenile literature. | Climatic changes–Juvenile literature.
Classification: LCC QH75.B77 2018 | DDC 639.9'2–dc23

Printed in the United States of America

CPSIA compliance information: Batch #CW18KL: For further information contact Greenhaven Publishing LLC, New York, New York at 1-844-317-7404.

Please visit our website, www.greenhavenpublishing.com. For a free color catalog of all our high-quality books, call toll free 1-844-317-7404 or fax 1-844-317-7405.

CONTENTS

Words in **bold** are explained in the glossary on page 31.

WHAT IS CLIMATE CHANGE?

KEY TERMS

- The <u>weather</u> is the day-to-day changes we see and feel outside. For example, the weather may be sunny in the morning and rainy in the afternoon.

- The <u>climate</u> is the usual weather in a place over a longer period of time. For example, Antarctica has an extremely cold climate for most of the year.

- <u>Climate change</u> is the long-term change in the climate and usual weather patterns of an area. Climate change usually affects large areas. It could be a change in the amount of rainfall or the average temperature of an area.

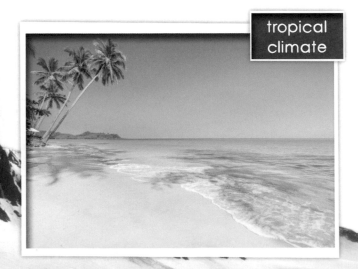

tropical climate

Earth's climate is always changing. Over the last 4.5 billion years, Earth has experienced both hot and cold climates. For the last 11,000 years, Earth's climate has stayed at a stable temperature of around 57° F (14° C). However, in recent years this average temperature has been slowly increasing.

arctic climate

Why Might a Climate Change?

There are many different reasons for why a climate might change.

Some climate changes throughout history have had natural causes, for example volcanic eruptions. However, research has shown that changes to the climate in recent years have not been entirely related to natural causes. It is thought that a process called global warming is largely responsible.

Humans use energy for many different reasons, for example to power cars and light bulbs. This energy is largely produced by burning coal, oil, and natural gas. Together, these things are known as **fossil fuels**. When these fossil fuels are burnt, they release many different gases, which are known as "greenhouse gases." One of the worst of these greenhouse gases is carbon dioxide.

Earth's **atmosphere** is a collection of different gases that surround the planet. The atmosphere allows light and heat from the sun to pass through to Earth. This makes the planet warm. After this, some of the light and heat from the sun bounce off Earth, travel back through Earth's atmosphere, and go into outer space.

Greenhouse gases mix with the gases in Earth's atmosphere and stop the heat from the sun bouncing back into outer space. Because of this, the heat gets trapped inside the Earth's atmosphere. As a result, the temperature on Earth is rising. The more greenhouse gases that are released into Earth's atmosphere, the hotter Earth will become.

WHAT IS A HABITAT?

A plant's or animal's habitat is their home; it's the place where they naturally live. An animal's habitat usually helps it to survive by providing it with food, water, shelter, and a safe place to raise its young. There are many different types of habitats around the world, such as ponds, woodlands, and jungles.

Each **species** of animal has **adapted** special traits over time that makes them better suited for their environment. An example of such an adaptation can be seen in the African elephant, which has huge ears that it uses to stay cool in the dry heat of the African savanna. The elephant's ears are covered in blood vessels that carry hot blood from inside the body. As the elephant flaps its ears, the breeze cools the blood, which then cools the elephant down.

A habitat can be large or small.

Since animals are so well-suited to their habitats, it can be difficult for them to survive in different places.

Some of the largest habitats in the world are in the ocean. Find out more about life under the sea on page 18.

Ecosystems

In every habitat there are many different animals and plants that must all **interact** with each other and with nonliving parts of the environment, such as the weather. This is an ecosystem. A healthy ecosystem relies upon energy being passed from plants to animals and between different species of animals. This is called a food chain.

| daffodil | caterpillar | frog | bird | fox |

This is an example of a food chain. The arrows point to the animal that feeds on the plant or animal in the previous stage.

It is important that ecosystems remain stable. If one part of an ecosystem is changed or disrupted, it can have an impact upon every **organism** in that ecosystem. For example, if the zebra's habitat in the African savanna was destroyed, the number of zebras would fall. With less zebras around, the number of lions would fall, as the big cats would have fewer animals to hunt. With less lions around, more animals might feel safe enough to live on the open savanna. This shows how changing one part of an ecosystem can lead to the whole ecosystem changing.

Within a habitat there can also be several microhabitats. Microhabitats are tiny habitats where small creatures and plants live. One habitat can be home to hundreds of microhabitats, each of which will have slightly different conditions than the larger habitat.

WHAT IS HABITAT DESTRUCTION?

Habitat destruction is when a habitat becomes unable to support the species living in it due to the habitat being changed or destroyed. As a result, the animals living in the habitat can find it difficult to survive. Both human and natural activity can be responsible for habitat destruction. Natural causes of habitat destruction include fires, floods, diseases, earthquakes, and volcanic activity; however, many areas can eventually recover from these natural events.

Changing a habitat does not always lead to the habitat being destroyed. Habitats are always changing, and, most of the time, they are able to deal with these changes. It is only when habitats change quickly, such as when huge areas of forest are cut down by humans, that they are unable to deal with the changes, leading to habitat destruction.

Some studies suggest that around 1 million different plant and animal species will become extinct in the next 50 years as a result of habitat destruction.

Habitat Fragmentation

A different type of habit destruction is called habitat fragmentation. Fragmentation happens when a habitat is altered but not completely destroyed. For example, if a road was built through the middle of a habitat, it could cut the habitat in half. The animals may choose to always stay on one side of the road, never crossing the road to look for food on the other side.

The International Union for Conservation of Nature (IUCN), an organization that tries to protect and **conserve** nature, has a list of species that it calls the "red list." All of the animals on this list are **endangered**, and habitat destruction is believed to be one of their biggest threats.

CLIMATE CHANGE AFFECT HABITATS?

Climate change has had a range of effects on animal habitats around the world.

Ice around the North and South Poles has been melting in recent years due to global warming. This has made it difficult for the animals that live in these habitats to survive.

The melting ice adds more water into the oceans. This increase of water raises the sea level and destroys beach habitats. This means that animals that nest on beaches will have nowhere to give birth to their young, meaning that they could quickly become endangered.

A sea turtle lays its eggs in a nest in the sand.

Climate change could also cause more extreme weather conditions. For some parts of the world, severe **droughts** are becoming increasingly common. Droughts can kill the plant life that animals rely on for their food and water. As a result, these areas can become **uninhabitable** and their ecosystems can be destroyed.

Animal Migration

Warmer temperatures on Earth have disrupted the **migration** patterns of thousands of animals. Birds are one of the most common types of animals to migrate, and they often use the temperature to tell them when they should begin their migration. The changes in Earth's temperature have caused migrating birds to begin their journeys at the wrong times. If birds migrate at the wrong time, they could end up arriving in their new habitat too soon.

Although animals can adapt to new environments over time, the effects of climate change are happening too quickly for animals to keep up. If the temperature on Earth rose by just over 3.6° F (2° C), approximately between 20 and 30 percent of all the animal and plant species on the planet would be at risk of extinction. Since 1880, the average temperature on Earth has risen by an estimated 1.53° F (0.85° C).

migrating birds

POLLUTION

*Pollution is the introduction of a harmful **substance** into an environment.*

Pollution comes in many different forms. Both human and natural causes can lead to pollution. Pollution is extremely damaging to life on Earth, and it is a leading cause of habitat destruction.

Air pollution, caused mainly by the burning of fossil fuels, contributes to the rising temperature on Earth. One direct result of this is the melting ice in the areas around the North and South Poles. The animals that live in these areas, such as polar bears and penguins, are finding it harder to survive as the size of their habitat becomes smaller. Polar bears hunt for food on the surface of the ice, but as the ice melts away, they have fewer places to hunt. This makes it more difficult for them to catch food.

A polar bear is shown here trying to hunt.

Smoke from chimneys is a type of pollution.

Acid Rain

Acid rain occurs as a result of pollution. This type of rain is a harmful type of rain that is made when gases from burning fossil fuels build up in Earth's atmosphere and combine with rainwater. The result of this is rain that is extremely harmful to natural environments. When acid rain falls on forests, it can damage or kill much of the plant life. If the acid rain falls into lakes, it can be extremely damaging for the animals and plants that live in the lake. It could even kill them. This could result in the complete destruction of the ecosystem within the habitat and around the lake.

Water is essential for plants and animals to survive; however, the quality of the water on Earth is getting worse as a result of pollution. As well as acid rain, man-made chemicals, garbage, and waste are being released into water sources all over the world, and, as a result, habitats are being damaged. When a habitat is damaged by water pollution, it makes it difficult for the animals that live there to find clean water to drink. This can lead to a lot of animals dying.

This forest has been damaged by acid rain.

water pollution

LAND DESTRUCTION

In the last 100 years, the population on Earth has risen by over 4 billion people. Each one of those people needs space to live and food to eat. As a result, large areas of land that were previously home to plant and animal life have been destroyed to make way for the building of new homes and **facilities**. More space is also needed for farmers to grow more food.

In order to make space for the growing population, large areas of forest and woodland have been cut down. Over the years, this has damaged or destroyed the habitats of hundreds of different animals and plants. This process is called deforestation. On top of this, many of the trees that are cut down are burnt as fuel, which adds to the planet's air pollution problem and global warming.

Nowadays, areas of woodland can quickly be torn down and replaced with houses and roads. Animals that previously lived in these areas, such as foxes, squirrels, and rabbits, are often forced to find new places to live that have food and are safe.

deforestation in Canada

Wetlands

marshes

Wetlands are areas that are covered by water for large parts of the year. Wetland areas include **marshes**, rivers, lakes, and ponds. These areas of land are home to a wide range of animals such as frogs, ducks, and insects. Wetlands are also used by migrating birds as a safe place to rest and feed before they continue their journey.

Many of the wetland areas around the world have been drained of their water and turned into spaces for farming or houses. Animals living in wetland areas need the water to survive, so, when the water is drained away, they are forced to move away from their habitat. If they are unable to find a new habitat quickly, they could die.

Plants need water to live. If the water is drained from wetland areas, the plant life that relied on this supply of water is also affected.

AROUND HALF OF THE WORLD'S WETLAND AREAS HAVE DISAPPEARED SINCE 1900.

FORESTS

Forests are home to millions of species of animal and plant life. Many endangered species live in forest habitats. As well as providing homes for a huge range of animals, forests also help to reverse the effects of climate change. Plants absorb carbon dioxide, which is one of the most damaging greenhouse gases. In return, the plants give off oxygen, which all animals need in order to survive.

Forests are home to many different animals and plants.

Deforestation is happening all over the world and at an extremely fast pace. While many countries around the world are trying to plant more trees, which is called **reforestation**, large areas of forest are still being lost every year. Deforestation has a huge impact on the area, and many animals cannot survive this immediate loss of habitat. Humans are nearly always the cause of deforestation, although fires do occasionally destroy large areas of woodland. The reason humans cut down such huge areas of forest is usually to collect the wood from the trees, which can be burnt as a fuel or used as building material. As well as this, the cleared land is often used for farming.

IT IS ESTIMATED THAT AN AREA OF FOREST THE SIZE OF 48 FOOTBALL FIELDS IS LOST EVERY MINUTE TO DEFORESTATION.

deforestation

The Amazon Rain Forest

The Amazon rain forest in South America is the world's largest tropical rain forest. The rain forest is believed to be home to 10 percent of all the animal species in the world. The rain forest is also home to over 40,000 different species of plants that thrive in the wet and hot conditions.

The Amazon has been badly affected by deforestation. In the last 40 years, an area of the Amazon rain forest the size of France has been lost due to deforestation. The deforestation has had devastating effects upon the ecosystems within the rain forest.

The removal of trees has also destroyed the rain forest's **canopy**. The canopy is important, as it blocks strong rays of sunlight during the day and helps to keep the forest warm during the night, which helps to maintain a stable temperature for the animals that live there. As more trees are removed, it becomes harder for the rain forest to maintain a stable temperature. This could make it difficult for the animals that live in the Amazon to survive.

UNDER THE SEA

Human activity is impacting life under the sea in many different ways. The most damaging of these is overfishing. Overfishing occurs when more fish are caught and removed from the sea than can be replaced through natural **reproduction**. As the population on Earth increases, so does the number of fish being caught. As a result, some species of fish, such as bluefin tuna, are now endangered species.

Some of the carbon dioxide that is released when fossil fuels are burnt gets absorbed into the ocean. Although this process helps to reduce the impact of carbon dioxide on the atmosphere, it has a damaging impact upon the ocean. As the carbon dioxide is absorbed, the water becomes more **acidic**. This process is called ocean acidification. An ocean that is more acidic than it should be could end up killing much of the plant and animal life that lives there.

Shown here is a fishing port in England.

PH 316

Coral Bleaching

Millions of species, including lobsters, clams, seahorses, and sponges, live near or in coral reefs. Coral reefs are typically colorful. However, the corals themselves are naturally white. The corals get their color from the **algae** that live on them. Algae are the coral's main food source, and without algae, the coral cannot survive. As the temperature on Earth increases, so too does the temperature of the ocean.

The increased temperature often makes the coral unwell and causes it to push away the algae. Without the algae to give it color, the coral is left white. This is why it is called coral bleaching. This process does not kill the coral right away, but if the warmer temperatures continue over a long period of time, the coral will eventually die. This would mean that the animals that live in the coral reef would have nowhere to live.

coral bleaching

The Great Barrier Reef, off the coast of Australia, is the largest coral reef in the world. It is so big that it can be seen from space! The Great Barrier Reef has experienced extreme coral bleaching events before. In 2002, 60 percent of the coral reef was bleached due to the warm weather. Although most of it did recover, about 5 percent never recovered.

Coral reefs are famous for their beautiful colors.

ASIAN ELEPHANTS

Asian elephants are found in many different countries in Asia, including India and Sri Lanka. They often live together in herds, meaning that they need a lot of space in which to live. Asian elephants prefer woodland areas with warm, dry weather. These elephants are **herbivores**, feeding mainly on the long grass that grows between trees, as well as bark, leaves, roots, and stems. They require as much as 330 pounds (150 kg) of food per day to survive and must also drink at least once a day, which means that fresh water sources within their habitat are extremely important.

Due to their size, elephants do not have any natural **predators**. Despite this, the number of Asian elephants left in the wild is rapidly decreasing. The Asian elephant is described on the IUCN red list as endangered, which is the second most severe status that can be given to a species and suggests that the animal is likely to become extinct. The fact that these elephants are endangered is largely the result of human activity.

> ASIAN ELEPHANTS ARE SIMILAR TO AFRICAN ELEPHANTS, EXCEPT THEY HAVE SMALLER EARS AND A SHORTER TRUNK.

India

Sri Lanka

An Asian elephant with its calf is shown here.

A large amount of the Asian elephant's habitat has been lost because humans have built settlements on the land. Areas of woodland have been torn down to make way for homes, roads, and services for the people who live in Asia. Much of the wood is taken away and used for fuel, while the long grass is removed or left to die. Wetlands are often filled in, meaning that sources of clean water are harder to find. All of this has meant that the Asian elephant's habitat has gotten a lot smaller and has become a lot harder to live in.

As a result of habitat destruction, Asian elephants now only inhabit 15 percent of the land that they used to live on. Elephants are sociable animals, but since their habitat has been made smaller and divided up by busy roads, herds of elephants have found it much more difficult to interact with each other.

THERE ARE ONLY BETWEEN 40,000 AND 50,000 ASIAN ELEPHANTS LEFT IN THE WILD. ALTHOUGH THIS NUMBER MAY SOUND LARGE, THERE WERE ROUGHLY TWICE THIS MANY ASIAN ELEPHANTS ALIVE 100 YEARS AGO.

CASE STUDY
MOUNTAIN GORILLAS

Mountain gorillas were first discovered in 1902. These gorillas have shorter arms than most apes, as well as thicker fur, which keeps them warm in the cold mountain areas that they call home. They live in dense forests that are high in the mountains. Mountain gorillas are found in two main locations: the Virunga Mountains in the Democratic Republic of the Congo, Rwanda, and Uganda and the Bwindi National Park in Uganda.

Mountain gorillas are herbivores, mostly eating bamboo, thistles, and fruit. The gorillas require a large amount of food due to their size. Mountain gorillas have an extremely slow rate of reproduction. Females can only give birth every three or four years and have just one baby at a time. As a result of this, if the population of mountain gorillas falls, it could take a long time to increase their numbers again.

Democratic Republic of the Congo (green), Rwanda (blue), and Uganda (red)

infant mountain gorilla

THE AVERAGE MALE MOUNTAIN GORILLA CAN WEIGH AS MUCH AS 352 POUNDS (160 KG)!

The number of mountain gorillas is not as high as it once was. The main reason for this is human activity, as more than 100,000 people now live on land that used to be part of the mountain gorillas' habitat. In 2004, over 3,700 acres (1,497 ha) of the gorillas' woodland habitat was cleared by people who wanted to build houses there. As more of the gorillas' habitat has been destroyed through deforestation, the gorillas have been forced to move further up the cold mountains.

A settlement on the Virunga Mountains in Uganda

The soil found in the Virunga Mountains is ideal for growing crops, and, because of this, much of this land has been claimed for farming and producing food. In addition to this, power companies are exploring the area hoping to find supplies of fossil fuels underground. Any discoveries could result in even more habitat loss for the gorillas.

AS A RESULT OF CONSERVATION WORK TO PROTECT WHAT IS LEFT OF THEIR NATURAL HABITAT, THE NUMBER OF WILD MOUNTAIN GORILLAS IS NOW BEGINNING TO INCREASE. FIND OUT MORE ABOUT CONSERVATION WORK ON PAGE 26.

Large areas of the Virunga Mountains are now used for farming.

WHAT HAPPENS WHEN A HABITAT IS GONE?

It is important that animal habitats are looked after so that no species is forced into extinction. Over time, natural events can cause many animals to go extinct. Forest fires can burn away huge areas of woodland, volcanic eruptions can destroy whole islands, and heat waves and ice ages can leave animals without enough food and water to survive. There will always be species that are about to go extinct, but we should do our best to protect them for as long as we can.

When an entire habitat is destroyed, the plants and animals that lived in that habitat are destroyed, too. The most common reasons for this happening include climate change, pollution, land destruction, **poaching**, and over-hunting. Together these things are putting a huge strain on life all over the planet. From polar bears in the Arctic to gorillas in Africa, all life on Earth is suffering because of the damage that humans have done, and are continuing to do, to the environment.

When a habitat has been destroyed, the surviving animals have to find somewhere else to live. These animals have no choice but to move into a new area, which can often have an effect on the animals that already live there. In some cases, the animals find it hard to survive, as the new habitat does not meet their needs.

Often the animals that are forced out of their habitat end up disrupting a different ecosystem, perhaps because they start to eat a food that another animal relied on. This is known as being **invasive**. Invasive animals can put a lot of strain on an ecosystem by eating up food sources that other species relied on. In some cases, invasive animals can lead to whole habitats and ecosystems being destroyed.

Shown here are bears hunting for salmon in Alaska.

bacteria cells

Diseases can infect plants and animals, but most animals have adapted defenses to fight off common diseases in their habitat. However, when an invasive animal arrives from a different habitat, they can bring with them new diseases. The animals that already live in the area may not have any defense against the new disease, meaning that many of them could die quickly.

25

HABITAT PROTECTION

The protection of animal habitats from any further destruction is important, and many groups around the world are working to achieve this. They work to protect areas of land and the endangered species living there.

National parks and reserves have been established worldwide to offer a safe place for animals to live. These areas of land are protected by law, meaning that deforestation, poaching, and building work are not allowed. Other areas, such as the Great Barrier Reef in Australia, have been protected by the same laws so that humans cannot fish or take naturally growing plant life from that area of the ocean. Some parks and reserves offer the opportunity for visitors to pay money to see the animals living there. This money goes toward maintaining the habitat.

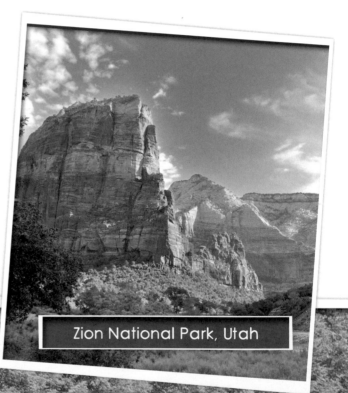

Zion National Park, Utah

Shown here are people rafting on the Tara River in Durmitor National Park, Montenegro.

The World Wide Fund for Nature, often just called WWF, was established in 1961. It is a conservation group, meaning it works to protect animal species and their habitats by trying to reduce the harm of human activities on the environment. The group works in over 100 countries, making it the biggest conservation group in the world.

The WWF does lots of different things in order to protect wildlife and habitats around the world. It supports **sustainable** methods of collecting wood, it helps to stop illegal or dangerous fishing, it promotes awareness of climate change and pollution, and it helps to fund conservation work around the world.

So far the WWF has run many successful campaigns to achieve these goals, such as reducing the amount of fishing in certain habitats, bringing a stop to companies looking for oil in the habitats of endangered species, and stopping lots of large-scale deforestation.

There are many other groups, such as Greenpeace, The Nature Conservancy, and Natural Resources Defense Council, who all work to protect wildlife and habitats from damage and destruction.

HOW CAN WE HELP?

There are many different ways that we can all help to stop habitat destruction.

 Try to find out about the wildlife and habitats in your local area and consider getting involved with local conservation groups.

Tell your family and friends about climate change and how important it is to look after our planet. Also, try to get as many people as you can interested in helping to save the environment.

 Recycle! It is important that we recycle as much as possible in order to reduce the amount of waste being put into landfill sites. Recycling can be done at home, at school, and in the wider community, so try to make sure that anything you can recycle is taken to special recycling banks or is put in recycling bins.

4 Try not to be wasteful. Food waste also contributes to the waste being dumped in landfill sites, so try to reuse anything that doesn't need to be thrown away and make sure that food is eaten before it goes out of date.

Try to reduce the amount of fossil fuels that you use. Rather than using the car, try to walk or ride your bike to where you need to go. If you have to use a car, try sharing with others who are also going to the same place. You could also turn down the heating at home and wear more layers of clothing to stay warm instead. **5**

6 Plant a tree! Trees absorb some of the greenhouse gases that cause climate change and give off oxygen. The more trees that are planted, the better!

The WWF holds "Earth Hour" every year. On the last Saturday in March, everyone who is taking part turns off the lights in their house for one hour between 8:30 p.m. and 9:30 p.m. The WWF hopes that this act will show how much people care about the planet. Why not join in and turn off your lights for an hour?

USEFUL WEBSITES

To find out more about the work of the WWF, go to: www.wwf.org. Click on the tab that says "get involved" to find out what you could do to help!

Visit www.iucn.org to discover how the IUCN helps to protect animal homes.

Learn how to better reduce, reuse, and recycle your garbage with this website: www.recycleguide.org.

Use this informative website climatekids.nasa.gov to learn all about climate change. Click on the "play" tab to play games as you learn.

Go to www.earthtimes.org for interesting blogs and pages that are filled with environmentally friendly ideas and tips.

To discover more about Greenpeace, visit www.greenpeace.org/usa.

Visit www.nature.org to find out about The Nature Conservancy. Go to the "where we work" section to find out about conservation work that's happening near you.

GLOSSARY

acidic	containing a lot of acid
adapt	to change over time to suit different conditions
algae	living things that are like plants, but have no roots, stems, leaves, or flowers
atmosphere	the mixture of gases that make up the air and surround Earth
canopy	the top layer of branches in a forest
conserve	to protect from damage or harm
drought	a long period of little rainfall, which leads to a lack of water
endangered	when a species of animal is in danger of becoming extinct
extinct	a species of animal that is no longer alive
facility	a building provided for a specific purpose
fossil fuel	a fuel, such as coal, oil, and gas, that formed millions of years ago from the remains of animals and plants
herbivore	an animal that only eats plants
interact	to be involved or communicate with another creature
invasive	spreading quickly and causing harm
marsh	ground near a river, a lake, or the sea that is always wet and often floods
migration	the seasonal movement of animals from one area to another
organism	a living thing
poach	to catch and kill animals without permission
predator	an animal that hunts other animals for food
reforestation	planting trees
reproduction	the process of having young
species	a group of similar animals or plants that are capable of producing young together
substance	something with physical properties
sustainable	able to continue over a period of time
uninhabitable	not suitable to live in

INDEX